ART PROFILES
For Kids

CANALETTO

P.O. Box 196
Hockessin, Delaware 19707
Visit us on the web: www.mitchelllane.com
Comments? email us: mitchelllane@mitchelllane.com

ART PROFILES FOR KIDS

Titles in the Series

Art Profiles
For Kids

CANALETTO

Earle Rice Jr.

Mitchell Lane
PUBLISHERS

P.O. Box 196
Hockessin, Delaware 19707
Visit us on the web: www.mitchelllane.com
Comments? email us: mitchelllane@mitchelllane.com

Copyright © 2008 by Mitchell Lane Publishers. All rights reserved. No part of this book may be reproduced without written permission from the publisher. Printed and bound in the United States of America.

Printing   1   2   3   4   5   6   7   8   9

Library of Congress Cataloging-in-Publication Data
Rice, Earle.
  Canaletto / by Earle Rice Jr.
      p. cm. — (Art profiles for kids)
  Includes bibliographical references and index.
  ISBN 978-1-58415-561-4 (library bound)
  1. Canaletto, 1697–1768—Juvenile literature. 2. Artists—Italy—Biography—Juvenile literature.
I. Title.
  N6923.C324R53 2007
  759.5—dc22
  [B]

2007023412

ABOUT THE AUTHOR: Earle Rice Jr. is a former senior design engineer and technical writer in the aerospace, electronic-defense, and nuclear industries. He has devoted full time to his writing since 1993 and is the author of more than fifty published books. Earle is listed in *Who's Who in America* and is a member of the Society of Children's Book Writers and Illustrators, the League of World War I Aviation Historians and its UK-based sister organization, Cross & Cockade International, the United States Naval Institute, the Air Force Association, and the Disabled American Veterans.

ABOUT THE COVER: The images on the cover are paintings by the various artists in this series.

PHOTO CREDITS: p. 17—Luca Carlevaris; p. 18—Antonio Visentini; p. 25—Bernardo Bellotto; p. 41—Barbara Marvis; all other artwork by Canaletto.

PUBLISHER'S NOTE: The facts on which this story is based have been thoroughly researched. Documentation of such research appears on page 47. While every possible effort has been made to ensure accuracy, the publisher will not assume liability for damages caused by inaccuracies in the data, and makes no warranty on the accuracy of the information contained herein.

Table of Contents

Art Profiles for Kids

Grand Canal: Looking East from the Campo San Vio is the first of four Venetian scenes by Canaletto known as the Liechtenstein quartet. Painted before 1723, its "dramatic" coloration reflects the influence of stage design on the artist's early works. A tiny section of the Campo San Vio appears in the lower right-hand corner of the picture.

First Steps

Owen McSwiney was a failed theatrical impresario in eighteenth-century Venice, Italy. The eccentric Irishman had not done well at producing plays and operas. Actually, he had done a whole lot less than well—he had gone bankrupt in London. To his credit, however, he was a cultured man of many ideas and interests. Next to his love for the performing arts, McSwiney felt strongly attracted to the world of fine arts. This attraction helped him recover from financial distress, and led him to Venice in 1711.

McSwiney settled in to the city called *La Serenissima*—"the Most Serene"—by Venetians. He became an agent for English producers and various art collectors. Through his business dealings, he developed a keen eye and deep appreciation for the works of many artists in Venice. Eleven years after his arrival there, McSwiney met a young artist with a superior talent. He saw the young man's potential at once and commissioned a parcel of work from him.

Describing the skills of his newly discovered painter in a contract for a series of paintings, McSwiney wrote, "His excellence lyes in painting things as they fall, immediately under his eyes."[1] What lay immediately under the young artist's eyes was a city built on a lagoon between the Italian mainland and the sea. With brush and palette, he captured images of the city that would represent how the world imagined Venice for centuries to come. The artist's name was Giovanni Antonio Canal. The world knows him better as Canaletto, painter of Venice.

Venice was unique among the great cities of Europe. Over centuries, it had been built up in a great lagoon on a cluster of islands and timber pilings.

Painted about 1723, the *Piazza San Marco: Looking East* demonstrates Canaletto's command of perspective. It is the second painting of a group of four owned by the Prince of Lichtenstein. Repaving of the famous square occurred about 1723/24 and so helps to date the painting accurately.

Interconnected by bridges and canals, a great metropolis emerged. The Republic of Venice reached its peak as the leading Mediterranean naval and commercial power during the fifteenth and sixteenth centuries. It ranked as the strongest city-state in Italy. A political leader known as the Doge headed its balanced government of councils. The councils were made up of nobles. Coupled with an impartial legal system, the Venetian government ensured domestic stability and set it apart from all others in Europe.

In the ninth century, Venetian traders smuggled relics of Mark the Evangelist out of Alexandria, Egypt, and brought them to Venice. The city adopted St. Mark as its patron saint. Over the years, his symbol—a winged lion—came to represent Venetian maritime supremacy. St. Mark's Basilica, the city's most famous building, attracted visitors year round. An adjoining square provided a public gathering place for ceremonial events.

Along the Grand Canal, tourists could view the palaces of nobility and visit public buildings such as the Ducal Palace, home of the Doge. At the Rialto, also on the Grand Canal, visitors could watch merchants scurrying about on business, and traders unloading their cargoes. Trade brought wealth and power to Venice.

By the eighteenth century, Venice's prominence among the great cities of Europe had largely declined, but its splendor—though faded—lived on. Venetians kept their zest for life. A six-month-long Carnival spoke to their carefree lifestyle. The city's festive atmosphere and numerous gambling casinos attracted many travelers. Its theaters and opera houses offered new life to a final flowering of the arts. More than a few musicians, composers,

actors, opera stars, writers, and artists found inspiration in the city of islands and canals. Of all the artists who drew inspiration from Venice, none gave back more to the city than Canaletto.

Canaletto began his life in a world of art and make-believe. He was born near the Campo San Lio in the heart of Venice on October 28, 1697. His family home on the Corre del Perini stood just a short distance from the Rialto Bridge. He would later make the arched span familiar to the world with his gifted brush.

Artistic talent ran in Canaletto's family. His father, Bernardo Canal, earned his living as a theatrical scene painter. Canaletto's brother, Cristoforo, also worked as a scene painter. Young Giovanni probably took the name Canaletto—meaning "little Canal"—to distinguish himself from his father. Bernardo was also a skilled landscape painter. Both Canaletto and Cristoforo took their early art training under him.

A birth certificate from the Church of Santa Maria Formosa names Artemisia Barbieri as Canaletto's mother. Little else is known of her. The Canals were listed as "original citizens" of Venice. This listing suggests that they enjoyed upper-class status. As an adult, Canaletto often used the family coat of arms—a blue goat's head on a silver background—as his signature. Despite his later fame, almost nothing is known of the artist's early life. Canaletto's recorded story begins about the time he joined his father and brother as a scene painter.

In 1716, Canaletto completed his first set designs on his own for two Venetian theaters, San Angelo and San Cassiano. From 1716 to 1718, Bernardo and his sons produced stage settings for various musical works in Venice. Beyond this period, history seems to have ignored what happened to Cristoforo. His future career went unrecorded.

In 1719, Canaletto went with his father to Rome. Together, they worked on set designs and scene paintings for two operas by Alessandro Scarlatti. The operas were to be performed for the Carnival in Rome in 1720. During this period, Canaletto tired of scene painting. He apparently fell under the sway of some eighteenth-century landscape painters and *vedutà* (vee-DOO-tah) artists, such as Gaspar van Wittel and Giovanni Paolo Pannini. (*Vedutà* means "view" in Italian and stands for a factually accurate landscape, generally

a cityscape.) Luca Carlevaris, an artist from Udine who was then nearing sixty, had helped to establish a market for *vedute* over his long career.

Apart from his work for the operas, Canaletto began painting landscapes and sketching the ruins of Rome. Anton Maria Zanetti, an Italian writer of Canaletto's time, noted that he "devoted himself entirely to painting views after nature."[2] Some of his sketches survived the years, but his paintings did not. Art historians believe that he used the sketches to produce paintings of Rome back in Venice some twenty years later. His experiments with landscapes strengthened his draftsmanship skills that would become so apparent in his later views of Venice. Around this time, he decided to take up *vedute* and renounce scene painting.

In 1720, Canaletto returned to Venice and applied for membership in the Fraglia dei Pittori, the Venetian painters' guild. His admission to the guild identified him as a master painter. He later declared that he had "solemnly excommunicated the theater."[3] At some point within the next two years, he signed his first contract with Owen McSwiney and used the nickname "Canaletto" for the first time.

McSwiney probably met Canaletto through Joseph Smith, an Englishman who would soon play a major role in advancing the artist's career. Smith was a man of many persuasions—banker, merchant, art collector, editor, and society figure. He later became the British consul in Venice. Many visitors learned the secrets of Venice as guests in Smith's lavish home. Unlike McSwiney, who was almost always in debt, Smith enjoyed great success in all of his varied undertakings. Smith, like McSwiney, quickly recognized Canaletto's talent. He slowly formed a close—and profitable—relationship with the artist.

Canaletto's first contract with McSwiney was for two paintings of imaginary tombs of great characters in recent English history. He apparently did not work for long on the project; demands from other patrons likely intervened. He painted the first of four views of Venice for another client sometime before 1723. Three others followed between 1723 and 1725. All four Venetian scenes displayed a master's eye for detail and an exceptional technical skill. At age twenty-eight, the former scene painter had taken his first steps toward becoming a *vedutista* (vee-doo-TEES-tah)—a painter of cityscapes.

The First Four

Art scholars generally believe that Canaletto painted his first four views of Venice for the Prince of Liechtenstein. They are sometimes referred to as the "Liechtenstein quartet." The paintings portrayed two views of the Grand Canal and individual views of the Piazza San Marco and the Rio dei Mendicanti. (See "Views of Venice," page 42.)

Canaletto titled the first of the four Venetian scenes *Grand Canal: Looking East, from the Campo San Vio.* The artist's almost theatrical treatment of this view of the canal from a campo (small square) dates it as the earliest of the four works. Scaffolding shown on the dome of the Church of Santa Maria della Salute in the right mid-distance indicates that the painting might have been done at the time of repairs to the dome in 1719.

The second painting, *Piazza San Marco: Looking East,* was probably painted in 1723. The Church of San Marco and the Campanile (bell tower) loom high in the center of the picture. Buildings of the Procuratie—the nine highest-ranking state officials—close off the square in a trapezoidal shape. A central vanishing point illustrates Canaletto's command of perspective. (Perspective is the method of representing three-dimensional objects on a flat surface to evoke a sense of depth.) Figures arranged in small groups or in pairs along the market stalls in the background give the square bustling vitality.

Canaletto completed the quartet with the *Grand Canal: From the Palazzo Balbi Toward the Rialto Bridge* and the *Rio dei Mendicanti* sometime between 1723 and 1725. In the first painting, he depicts the Grand Canal at its widest point. His composition and use of two light sources reflect the continuing influence of his experience with set design. Canaletto's use of chiaroscuro (kee-ahr-uh-SKYUR-oh)—strongly con-

trasting light and shade—in the last painting lends a certain intimacy and mystery to a poor section of Venice. At a time when most artists focused on ideal beauty, his choice of the Mendicanti district as a subject was considered unusual. It may have been his way of distancing himself from the influence of other artists of his time, such as Luca Carlevaris.

Rio dei Mendicanti, the last painting in the Liechtenstein group, represents a study in light and shadow. It depicts a moody view of Venice's poor section.

The Stonemason's Yard is acclaimed by many art critics as one of the high points in Canaletto's early works. As the artist matured, his canvases became flooded with glittering light and captured the Venetian scene in all its characteristic luminosity. Against a background of the church of Santa Maria della Clarita across the Grand Canal, the painting focuses on the everyday activities of working people in the foreground.

The Early Phase

Like all artists, Canaletto drew inspiration from other artists of his time and from those who came before him. Two artists who influenced him greatly were the Dutch painter Gaspar van Wittel and Luca Carlevaris from Udine, Italy. Art scholars often credit van Wittel for starting the trend toward *vedute* among Venetian artists. Italians knew him as "Vanvitelli." He did most of his work while living in Rome, but he visited Venice briefly. He probably had some influence on Carlevaris, who was highly active in Venice. The work of both artists strongly affected the development of the younger Canaletto.

Art agents often likened Canaletto's early work to that of Carlevaris. For example, art collector Stefano Conti of Lucca owned three Carlevaris paintings. About 1725, he wanted to add two more to his collection. He called on agent Alessandro Marchesini in Venice to obtain them, but Marchesini instead suggested a new artist. Canaletto, he told Conti, was astounding everyone who saw his work: "It is like that of Carlevaris, but you can see the sun shining in it."[1] Conti ordered not two but four Canaletto paintings.

During the last half of the 1720s, Canaletto achieved almost instant success. The five-year period was marked by intense activity. Art scholars regard it as a time in which his research led to his "conquest of light"[2] that would illuminate all his future works. This breakthrough in the effects of light does not yet "shine through" in the Conti paintings, which Canaletto painted in 1725–1726. In four views of the Grand Canal, his free and dense brushwork retains his fascination with chiaroscuro.

In a first sketch of the Rialto Bridge for the first painting, Canaletto wrote and underlined the word *sun* in ink where its effect was strongest and most

The Piazza: Looking North, the Campanile under Repair. Rendered in pen and ink with wash on paper in 1745, Canaletto's splendid drawing records in faithful detail the damage done to the Campanile on St. George's Day, April 23, 1745. Joseph Smith, the artist's patron and English cunsul to Venice, likely arranged its commission. The thousand-year-old bell tower ultimately collapsed 157 years later.

dazzling. His notation underscored his growing interest in the realistic rendering of natural light. It also bore out Marchesini's claim that Canaletto "always goes to the place, and fashions everything from life."[3] Painting *sopra il loco*—on the spot—was rare at a time when most artists worked in their studios from sketches made at the scene.

What Marchesini failed to point out was that Canaletto sketched his subjects on the spot with the aid of a camera obscura (KAM-er-uh ob-SKYUR-uh). Then, much like his fellow artists, he would complete the paintings in his studio. Art historians like to point out that many artists of the time used a camera obscura to lay out their compositions. A camera obscura is an instrument much like today's photographic cameras. Its name means "dark chamber" in Latin. It consists of a box with a small hole in one wall. A lens in the hole focuses on the scene outside and projects an upside-down image of the scene onto a system of angled mirrors. The mirrors reflect a right-side-up image onto a flat surface. This allowed the artist to trace a corrected image.

Though Canaletto used the device, he often corrected flaws in the image. He also altered its perspective to enhance artistic expression. This led later

critics to scold him for straying outside "the limits of the rules of perspective."[4] At the same time, they admitted that no one could rival him in "representing objects with more liveliness, or to greater effect."[5] Critics today concede that the camera obscura and other devices—rulers, dividers, and so on—played only a minor role in Canaletto's body of work. Rather than seeking the perfection of reality, Canaletto sought the *impression* of reality.

Beginning about 1726, Canaletto's paintings grew brighter and more flooded with light. He grew more adept at capturing Venice's *arie*—its light and atmosphere. Glittering canals reflected the sunshine and turned the city aglow in radiant light. His brushstrokes became delicate and well placed. He seemed suddenly able to turn forms and colors on canvas into real houses, palaces, canals, and small squares. Critics acclaimed his almost photographic images as wholly convincing. His artist's eye focused on outdoor views of Venetian architecture. His subjects consisted of the piazzas, narrow streets, canals, the Grand Canal, and views of St. Mark's.

Some consider *The Stonemason's Yard,* painted before 1730, to be Canaletto's masterpiece. It depicts the public face of the city. Canaletto looks down on a quiet square across the Grand Canal toward the Santa Maria della Carità, and small dramas of everyday life come alive at the tip of his brush. A mother rushing to aid her fallen child, a woman spinning on a nearby balcony, wisps of chimney smoke, and a glimpse of workers inside the stonemason's shed lend the illusion of reality to this scene.

As a rule, Canaletto developed his paintings from sketches drawn on the spot. He generally turned these first sketches into two types of worked-up drawings. One type provided working information to form a bridge between first thoughts and a completed painting or print. A second type contained great detail. Roughly 500 of Canaletto's drawings have survived.

Although Canaletto's drawings are less known than his paintings, they deserve recognition in their own right. They furnish important clues to the artist's methods. Drawing most often with pen and ink over pencil, Canaletto used wash or hatching to achieve tonal change. (Wash is diluted ink or transparent watercolor on paper; hatching is the use of finely spaced parallel lines to suggest shading.) In many of his drawings, these techniques produced highly sophisticated results that appeared much simpler to the eye.

Canaletto often added notes on coloring and detailed descriptions to his sketches. He used such notations to help him remember things he wanted to include in the finished painting. Some notes applied to an entire composition; others provided details of certain buildings. Still others suggested where to place staffage—small figures and animals that are not essential to the subject but that help to animate the composition. When transferring a composition to canvas, Canaletto sometimes changed it slightly. At other times, he sketched a subject from different viewpoints and combined several studies in a single painting. Combined studies produced magnificent "wide-angle" effects similar to stage settings. These effects were enhanced by the size of the canvas—the larger the canvas, the greater the effect.

Canaletto occasionally painted on copper, but he did most of his work on canvas. He prepared the canvas with a "ground," that is, a lower layer of paint that provides a smooth working surface. The hue and tone of this base layer affects the appearance of the finished picture. Canaletto used several grounds during his career. They tended to be dark in his early paintings, but were tinted with creams, ochres, and pinks in later works.

Once the ground was applied, Canaletto would sketch in his composition and begin to build it up. First, he would block in large areas of color, such as the sky or watery expanses. Next, he would outline buildings, often using rulers and dividers. Then, he would define details and textures. A few deft brushstrokes here might add a chimney pot and a plume of smoke over a patch of sky. Another few strokes there and a tiny figure might appear at an apartment window. Canaletto used both natural and man-made pigments. Mixing them with oil, he applied paint with a fairly heavily loaded brush. His rich, clear colors combined with sharply defined outlines of structures to create paintings that resonated with lifelike clarity.

By the end of the 1720s, Canaletto had completed a generous body of work. Scholars believe that he painted twenty canvases for Owen McSwiney alone between 1726 and 1730. However, only two have been positively identified. At some uncertain point before his early stage ended, his work attracted the attention of Joseph Smith. The suave man-about-Venice became Canaletto's patron and friend. For the next decade, Canaletto never lacked work.

Luca Carlevaris

Among the artists who directly influenced Canaletto, perhaps none stands out more than Luca Carlevaris. (His name is also spelled Carlevarijs.) He was born in 1663 in the northeastern Italian town of Udine. He preceded Canaletto by some thirty-four years. In addition to being a painter, he was also an engraver and an architect. Art scholars regard him as the father of eighteenth-century Venetian view painting.

Carlevaris was not the first to specialize in the *veduta* art form, but he used his mathematical training to bring new precision to his difficult perspective settings. Like Canaletto in the next generation, he was the son of a painter and designer. His father died when he was very young. In 1679, he moved from Udine to Venice, where he became the first painter of any significance to paint views of that city.

The wealthy Zenobio family discovered Carlevaris in Venice. Between 1682 and 1688, he painted large landscapes for their *palazzo* (mansion). He later visited Rome, where he probably became familiar with the works of view painters and *capricci* (kah-PREE-chee) artists such as Gaspar van Wittel. (*Capriccio* means "caprice" in Italian; it is used to define an imaginary but realistic-looking view.) When he returned to Venice in 1698, he established himself as a painter of similar works.

Carlevaris published an important series of 104 *veduta* etchings dating from 1703. Most of them depicted frontal views of important buildings and squares in Venice. This collection represented the first Venetian *vedute* conceived as a whole entity. He produced his first *veduta* painting sometime after 1703. Before then, his main output was probably consisted of *capricci* and landscapes.

Although scholars often regard Canaletto as a pupil of Carlevaris, no evidence supports that assertion. His only true pupil was a little-known artist named Johan Richter. Beyond question, however, Carlevaris greatly influenced the work of Canaletto and other eighteenth-century view painters.

The Bridge for the Feast of the Madonna della Salute, painted by Luca Carlevaris in 1720, shows Venetians crossing the Grand Canal on a temporary boat bridge.

Giovanni Antonio Canal, called Canaletto, an engraving of the artist done by Antonio Visentini before 1745. Visentini, born in Venice in 1688, was an eighteenth-century artist who specialized in wall decorations and easel paintings. He also designed houses, including two for Joseph Smith. Visentini is best remembered as an engraver, however, particularly for his engravings of Canaletto's paintings.

Good Times and Bad

Soon after Canaletto completed the four Conti paintings, Owen McSwiney came back into his life. He wanted some small views of the city painted on copper for English clients. Despite a heavy workload, Canaletto agreed to do two small paintings on copper. These were very different from his larger earlier canvases. (His view of the Grand Canal looking toward the Rialto Bridge, for example, measures 144 by 207 centimeters, or 56.7 by 81.5 inches.) McSwiney rightly believed that his English clients would prefer something smaller to hang on their walls to remind them of the Venice of their travels.

Canaletto later fell behind in delivering two such paintings for the Duke of Richmond. McSwiney wrote to him, explaining his problems in dealing with Canaletto: "He's a very difficult person, and changes his prices every day; and if one wants a picture from him, he should be very careful not to seem too anxious, because he risks losing out in terms both of price and quality. Canaletto has many more commissions than he should accept."[1] McSwiney's criticism of the artist did not stop there.

Three years later, in a letter to London client John Conduitt, McSwiney wrote of Canaletto: "He's a greedy and covetous man, and, being very famous, people are happy to pay him whatever he wants."[2] These letters indicate that Canaletto had become very busy and well known by the early 1730s. They also suggest McSwiney's displeasure at being unable to get what he wanted from the artist. McSwiney was not alone in his disapproval of Canaletto.

Count Tessin of Sweden, who visited Venice in 1736, described Canaletto as a greedy show-off. He stopped just short of calling him a swindler. Even

Joseph Smith, who represented Canaletto with wealthy visitors to Venice, once wrote of him: "This is not the first time that I have had to submit to the impertinence of a painter for my own interests or those of my friends."[3] In Canaletto's defense, many of his wealthy patrons tried to acquire his highly specialized paintings for little or nothing. He rarely got paid what he asked for a painting. And despite Smith's complaint, he stood loyally by the artist in both good times and bad during their long relationship.

Canaletto's failure to deliver the two small paintings for the Duke of Bedford seems to have ended his association with McSwiney. Or it just might have been that his new ties with Joseph Smith kept him too busy to accept work requests from other agents. Because so little has been documented about Canaletto's life and career, art historians cannot reliably date many of his paintings. Some scholars think that Smith's involvement with Canaletto began earlier than 1730. In any case, Canaletto's greatest productivity with Smith came between 1730 and 1740. The death of rival Luca Carlevaris in 1730 no doubt did little to lessen the demand for Canaletto's work.

Canaletto's first work for Smith consisted of a set of six paintings of the Piazzetta and the nearby area. (The Piazzetta is a small square near St. Mark's Square.) He painted the Venice known well by Venetians. The city's shabby and cluttered side showed through clearly under moody, threatening skies. His views did not much resemble the clean, sunny Venice that visitors might want to recall. Nor did they represent the type of painting that McSwiney— and later Smith—would want to order for sale to tourists. After the first six paintings of Venice's seamier side, Smith prompted Canaletto to focus on pictures depicting the "splendor" of Venice. Splendor no doubt sold better than squalor to Smith's foreign clients.

In the 1730s, Englishmen commissioned most of Canaletto's work through Smith. The Duke of Bedford ordered twenty-four paintings showing every aspect of Venice. Another twenty-one views of the Grand Canal, squares, and churches went to the Duke of Buckingham. As early as 1730, Smith advised one client that Canaletto was "so much followed and all are so ready to pay his own price for his work"[4] that only by using tact and patience could he hope to get anything out of him. In both Canaletto's interest and his own, Smith could not allow the artist to price himself out of buyers.

A series of pictures painted for Smith contained twelve views of the Grand Canal. Canaletto's tour of the Canal began with the *Grand Canal: Looking South-West from the Rialto Bridge to the Palazzo Foscari* and ended with the *S. Chiara Canal: Looking North-West from the Fondamenta della Croce to the Lagoon*. (S. stands for "Saint"; *Fondamenta della Croce* means "Foundation of the Cross" in Italian.) These paintings show the artist at the height of his powers, expressing the city's gentle serenity. Similar scenes occur in the series of twenty-four paintings for the Duke of Bedford. Both series included views of the artist's first portrayals of events celebrating Venice's past glories.

The Bucintoro Returning to the Molo marks Ascension Day festivities. It depicts the return of the Doge from the Lido after the ceremony of the Marriage of the Sea. (The *Bucintoro* was the state barge, propelled by 200 oarsmen; the Lido is an island reef where the waters of the Adriatic Sea

The Bucintoro Returning to the Molo, 1732. Canaletto painted this often-repeated view of the Molo and the Doge's Palace to capture the colorful festivities of Ascension Day. This celebration of one of Venice's past glories features the Doge's return from the Lido (island reef) after the ceremony of the Marriage of the Sea.

View of the Bacino di S. Marco, 1730–1735. Canaletto made numerous copies of his more famous subjects, usually to meet the demands of his many English clients. St. Mark's Basin and the Doge's Palace appear in a number of his paintings.

enter the Lagoon of Venice; and the Molo is the walkway along the Grand Canal outside the Doge's Palace. The wedding of Venice to the sea celebrates Venice's victory over Dalmatia in about the year 900. It also symbolizes the city's naval supremacy in its wonder years.

In *The Doge Visiting the Church and Scuola di San Rocco*, Canaletto honors the Feast Day of St. Roch. He painted the festival marking Venice's deliverance from the plague in 1576 only once. The painting shows the Doge and city officials leaving the church and walking past the *scuola* (school). At the time Canaletto committed the scene to canvas, the threat of the dreaded bubonic plague still lingered as a fearsome presence in the lives of Venetians. His painting seems to emphasize the real meaning of the event. Art scholars consider it to be one of the great masterpieces of the "Smith period."

In 1735, Joseph Smith published a book of fourteen engravings after paintings by Canaletto. He named it *Prospectus Magnus Canalis Venetiarum*,

or *Views of Venice's Grand Canal*. An artist named Antonio Visentini did the engravings. The title page made it clear that the paintings resided " 'in Aedibus Josephi Smith, Angli,' in the house of Joseph Smith, Englishman."[5] Initially, the book contained twelve views of the Grand Canal and two regatta scenes. In 1742, Smith issued a new edition with twenty-four new engravings added to the original fourteen. The additions showed ten more views of the Grand Canal, two of the Molo, ten of churches and their courts, and two of the Piazza San Marco.

Although most of Canaletto's commissions came through Smith in the 1730s, he also accepted work from other clients. He painted *The Bacino di S. Marco: Looking East* as one of a series for the earls of Carlisle. (St. Mark's Basin is the stretch of water into which the Grand Canal flows.) Canaletto probably painted this wide-angle view from several raised perspectives in 1738. It ranks high among his finest creations.

Because Canaletto produced so many paintings during the 1730s, some historians suspect that he must have used studio assistants. Artists of his time routinely used the help of apprentices. Their tasks included preparing canvases for painting, filling in backgrounds, and taking care of similar, less demanding work. Canaletto's nephew, Bernardo Bellotto, studied under him and might have served as his assistant. His father might also have helped out in the studio. Beyond these two, any evidence of an organized studio of assistants has yet to surface. Canaletto, it seems, was just remarkably prolific.

Canaletto's fame no doubt grew as a result of the reissued volume of engravings. Several Roman scenes dated 1742 clearly bear his signature. Five of them were painted for Joseph Smith. Art experts still wonder whether Canaletto painted them from life or from sketches he had made as early as 1720. He might have also worked from sketches of Rome provided by his nephew Bellotto.

In 1740, the War of the Austrian Succession broke out upon the death of Holy Roman Emperor Charles VI. Canaletto did not know it at the time, but the war would later have a profound effect on his career. Meanwhile, from 1741 to 1742, Canaletto traveled to the mainland and down the Brenta Canal to Padua. His nephew went with him. For a while, he seems to have put his

Piazza San Marco: Looking East from the South-West Corner, 1760. In this drawing, Canaletto rendered the famous square on paper in pen and ink with washes. The artist often drew over pencil with pen and ink. He used wash to achieve tonal changes.

painting aside. He instead devoted his energies to ink-and-wash drawings and etchings.

Between 1741 and 1744, Canaletto issued a series of etchings. He dedicated them to Joseph Smith, who became the British consul to Venice in 1744. The series comprised thirty-five mostly large etchings, some "copied from life, others imagined."[6] These included many views of locations close to St. Mark's Square. But Canaletto took elements from life and combined them with others of fancy to create *capricci.*

While Canaletto roamed the Brenta Valley with Bernardo Bellotto, the War of the Austrian Succession had spread to Italy in 1742. Its effects severely reduced the number of English visitors to Venice. Two years later, Bernardo Canal died, and Canaletto's career had begun to suffer. By mid-decade, the demand for Canaletto's work had fallen off drastically. Fortunately for him, talent is mobile. If customers could not come to him, he could go to them. In 1746, Canaletto left Venice for England. He would spend most of the next ten years there.

Bernardo Bellotto

Not one but three artists went by the name of Canaletto. The first to use the name was, of course, Giovanni Antonio Canal. He used the name meaning "little Canal" to distinguish himself from his father, Bernardo Canal. Bernardo was also an artist. He sometimes signed his paintings as "Canaletto" to trade on his son's fine reputation as an artist. Canaletto's artist nephew Bernardo Bellotto also used the diminutive nickname for much the same reason when working outside of Italy.

Bernardo Bellotto came closest to matching his uncle's enormous talents. He was born to Lorenzo Antonio Bellotto and Canaletto's eldest sister, Fiorenza Canal, in Venice in 1720. Bernardo entered his uncle's studio as an assistant about 1735. Three years later, the Venetian painters' guild accepted him as a member. He began accepting work orders from Joseph Smith and other art agents.

By 1740, Bellotto had developed into a full-fledged artist. Art experts describe his work in the studio as exhibiting a greater contrast between light and shade than that of his master and a thicker application of paint—in short, a heavier brush. His shadows appeared darker and colder in tone and color. Like his uncle, he used the camera obscura as an aid to achieving precision in his urban views.

In 1742, Bellotto moved to Rome and painted *vedute* of the city. On the invitation of King August III of Poland, he moved to Dresden. From 1747 to 1758, he painted views of Dresden and Pirna and their surroundings in Germany. Many of these paintings preserved the lost beauty of Dresden, which was destroyed by bombings in World War II.

The Moat of the Zwinger in Dresden, painted by Bernardo Bellotto (1749–1753), obscures the Zwinger Palace—a marvel of Baroque architecture—behind trees to one side, and focuses chiefly on the moat and other structures.

Beginning in 1758, Bellotto traveled about central Europe, painting cityscapes in Vienna, Munich, Dresden again, and then in St. Petersburg. In 1767, he accepted the offer of King Stanislaw II of Poland to become his court painter. His paintings of Warsaw were used to rebuild the city after its near destruction in World War II. Bellotto died there in 1780.

Detail of *London: The Thames and the City of London from Richmond House*, 1747. Canaletto painted one of his first paintings in London from Richmond House, the home of the Duke of Richmond. The duke's home offered marvelous views of the city. The painting's panoramic span brings to mind the artist's treatment of St. Mark's Basin, with an overlay of Venetian sunshine to brighten the grayer tones of the city on the Thames.

CHAPTER 4
four

The Artist Abroad

By 1745, Canaletto's clients had gradually fallen off to few and none. The War of the Austrian Succession had effectively shut down the flow of English travelers to the city of canals. At the urging of Jacopo Amigoni, Canaletto decided to take his brush and palette abroad. Amigoni was a fellow Venetian artist. He had earned a good living while working in England off and on from 1730 to 1739. Canaletto no doubt felt he could do the same. He might have also felt the need for new vistas to bring to canvas. More likely, though, his concerns sprang mostly from an artist's innate fear of hunger.

Once again, Joseph Smith came forward to help Canaletto. Smith wrote to Owen McSwiney, who had been back in London for about ten years. McSwiney apparently agreed to help Canaletto find new clients in England. Smith wisely did not refer the artist to his own clients, as they had all had ample opportunities to buy Canaletto paintings. Fortified with a letter of introduction from Joseph Smith, the famous Venetian view painter arrived in London in May 1746.

A letter to the Duke of Richmond from Thomas Hill, his former tutor, announced Canaletto's coming to the duke, who was out of town: "The only news I know to send you is what I had this day from [Mc]Swiney . . . Canales, alias Canaletti [sic], is come over with a letter of recommendation from our old acquaintance the Consul of Venice [Smith] to Mac [McSwiney] in order to [have] his introduction to your Grace. . . . I told him the best service I thought you could do him would be to let him draw a view from your dining-room, which in my opinion would give him as much reputation as any of his Venetian prospects."[1]

Meanwhile, Canaletto took up residence with a cabinetmaker named Wiggins in Silver Street, at what is now 41 Beak Street, Soho. (Soho is a district south of Oxford Street in the British capital; it has long been known as a foreign quarter and noted for its restaurants and shops.) Canaletto would live there during his entire stay in England. The house now bears a plaque recording his stay there.

Shortly after Canaletto had settled in to his new home, McSwiney greeted the artist warmly and introduced him to the Duke of Richmond. The duke became a great admirer of Canaletto's work and admitted him into his London residence, Richmond House. Canaletto painted one of his first London pictures from the house, which offered a marvelous view of the city.

London: The Thames and the City of London from Richmond House shows a panoramic view that brings to mind the artist's treatment of St. Mark's Basin. Its brilliant color and clarity suggests that Canaletto overlaid the sunny Venetian climate onto the grayer tones of the city on the Thames. After seeing the painting, the duke commissioned him to paint several more pictures. Later paintings would include further views of London—toward Whitehall and the Privy Garden, as well as another view of the Thames and the inner city of London. (Whitehall is a road in Westminster, London, where government offices are located; the Privy Garden is the king's private garden at London's Hampton Court Palace.) But the duke was not Canaletto's only client.

About that time, Canaletto, apparently by chance, came to know Prince Lobkowicz of Bohemia. (Bohemia was once a kingdom in central Europe; it now forms a part of the Czech Republic.) The prince was visiting England in the summer of 1746 to buy breeding stock for his racing stable. English author Horace Walpole described the prince as "a travelling boy of twenty . . . under the care of an apothecary [druggist] and surgeon."[2] Prince Lobkowicz commissioned—or at least bought—several paintings from Canaletto. Art scholars believe them to be Canaletto's very first paintings in England. The prince took them home with him to Bohemia, where they remain to this very day.

During his first two years abroad, Canaletto seems to have focused mainly on engravings and printed graphics for publishers. Publications

represented a quick way to become noticed in England. As word of his presence in England spread, his clients grew.

In 1747, Canaletto met Sir Hugh Smithson, later the Duke of Northumberland. The duke was one of the owners of the new Westminster Bridge, which was then under construction. Canaletto agreed to do a painting of the bridge for him. In *London, Seen Through an Arch of the Westminster Bridge*, one of the bridge's wooden arches forms a semicircular frame through which the viewer looks out upon the Thames, Westminster Abbey, and the surrounding city. The painting clearly shows that Canaletto's interest lay more in presenting an interesting composition and viewpoint than in depicting the bridge itself. Nonetheless, Sir Hugh liked it so much he commissioned a painting of Windsor Castle.

That same year, Canaletto probably completed *The Chapel of Eton College*. In the painting, he exaggerates the size of the chapel in the center

In *London Seen Through an Arch of the Westminster Bridge*, painted in 1747 for Sir Hugh Smithson (later the Duke of Northumberland), Canaletto used one of the bridge's wooden arches to frame a sweeping view of London on the Thames.

The Chapel of Eton College, 1747. The massive Gothic architecture and huge proportions of the Eton Chapel attract the viewer's eye and seize the painting's focal point. A larger-than-life depiction of the chapel, coupled with a less-than-accurate portrayal of the surrounding rural countryside, lends a mysterious *capriccio* effect to the artist's vision.

background. This overstatement lends a touch of *capriccio* to an otherwise realistic rural scene. His use of numerous small figures in everyday situations in the foreground brings the picture to life.

During those first years in England, it appears that Canaletto did quite well. From 1749 onward, he could count several English noblemen as clients. He painted views of Badminton House for the Duke of Beaufort and a picture of Warwick Castle for Lord Brooke. Despite his seeming success in England, not everyone sang his praises. George Vertue, an antiques dealer and engraver, stood at the forefront of Canaletto's detractors.

Vertue, who at the time was collecting material for a history of English art, flatly declared that he was not impressed by Canaletto's work in England: "[O]n the whole of him something is obscure or strange. He does not produce works so well done as those of Venice or other parts of Italy which are in collections here."[3] Out of professional jealousy or resentment over the

competition posed by the Venetian, English artists also began to criticize Canaletto's offerings. Vertue went on to note that Canaletto "is not the veritable Cannelleti [sic] of Venice . . . he has some unknown assistant in makeing [sic] up . . . his works with figures."[4]

A rumor that Canaletto was an impostor was taking on public acceptance. Vertue even went so far as to name Bernardo Bellotto as the real painter of Canaletto's English *vedute*. Bellotto was in central Europe at the time. He in fact never even set foot in England. Amid the increasing storm of false accusations and criticism, Canaletto felt the need to defend himself. He inserted paid advertisements in the *Daily Advertiser* in 1749 and again in 1751, inviting art lovers to his studio for public demonstrations of his skills. To doubters, he offered his painting of *London: the Old Horse Guards from St. James Park* as proof that he was the "real" Canaletto. Despite his difficulties, he continued to turn out painting after painting, producing more than fifty large canvases. Many of them still remain in the homes of noblemen.

In 1749, the Dean of Westminster Abbey commissioned Canaletto to capture the procession of the Knights of Bath for posterity. Other commissions followed, but in 1751, for some unclear reason, Canaletto returned to Venice. He also may have traveled home again briefly in 1753, but then remained in England until 1755. While in Venice, he bought a house on the Zattere, a long quay overlooking the Giudecca Canal and St. Mark's Basin. The artist was perhaps looking ahead to his retirement, which might explain his visit home.

Around the middle of 1751, Canaletto returned to his rented apartment on Silver Street in London. Many of his clients had deserted him. Two

London: the Old Horse Guards from St. James Park, 1753. Canaletto may have painted this scene to preserve the appearance of the Old Horse Guards building at the center of this work. The old building was demolished and replaced by the New Horse Guards building soon after Canaletto completed this painting.

The Old Walton Bridge was one of six paintings commissioned by Thomas Hollis, a friend of Joseph Smith. It represents another example of the artist's ability to take a real-life subject and cast a *capriccio*-like spell over it. Canaletto himself can be seen in the painting's left-center foreground as the seated artist.

remained loyal: Lord Brooke commissioned another view of Warwick Castle in 1752, and that same year, Sir Hugh Smithson, now the Duke of Northumberland, ordered several views of his country estates, including *Northumberland House*.

During the artist's remaining years in London, Thomas Hollis, a friend of Joseph Smith, ordered six paintings. They included a view of the *Old Walton Bridge* and another of the Westminster Bridge. Hollis himself appears in the foreground of the Walton Bridge painting, along with his servant, a friend, and his dog. Parliament member Samuel Dicker liked the Walton Bridge picture so much that he ordered another painting of it.

By the mid-1750s, Canaletto's time abroad was drawing to an end. At some point between 1755 and 1756, the artist departed England for Venice, this time for good. At almost sixty years of age, he left behind a splendid pictorial record of England in the Georgian era. He also left a lasting impression on English view painters—and he was not finished yet.

Westminster Bridge

The Westminster Bridge was a source of great controversy both before and during the building process. Opponents of a new bridge resisted its construction. They feared it would raise the water level of the Thames and flood out structures on its banks. It might also, they said, cause a silt buildup in the river and render it unnavigable for water traffic. Nonetheless, British lawmakers authorized its construction in 1736.

When completed, the new Westminster Bridge would connect Westminster and Lambeth in London and become a companion to the existing London Bridge. On January 29, 1739, the first stone, weighing about a ton, was sunk in mid-river and construction began on the new bridge. It was nearing completion about the time Canaletto arrived in London in May 1746.

Even while under construction, the bridge provided a prime subject for an artist of Canaletto's ability. Working on his own—or possibly commissioned by the Prince of Bohemia—Canaletto painted *London: The Thames, with Westminster Bridge in the Distance*. The painting was one of his first after arriving in England. Its sweeping vista of the river and the city shows the completed bridge as the painting's centerpiece. A second painting that year, titled *London: Westminster Bridge from the North on Lord Mayor's Day*, shows the finished bridge from the opposite direction. Canaletto obviously relied on a bit of artistic license in his rendering of the bridge in both paintings, as the bridge was not completed until at least two years later. It opened to the public in 1750.

In *London: The Thames Looking Toward Westminster from Near York Water Gate*, a view done in pen and brown ink with gray wash, Canaletto showed the half-completed bridge from the Westminster side, ending in mid-river. This was pure invention, because construction on the bridge was begun in the middle and worked toward both banks from midstream. Since art dealers lauded Canaletto for his accurate paintings from life, these works further added to the controversies surrounding the Westminster Bridge.

Photograph of the Westminster Bridge

Capriccio: Ruins and Classic Buildings. The art of *capriccio* combines real and imagined elements to create a fantasy landscape. Canaletto's *capricci* are difficult to identify, or even to date accurately, because he purposely departed from his usual work practices, using his imagination to deliver a mild shock to the viewer. This painting, though generally attributed to Canaletto, may have been painted by his nephew, Bernardo Bellotto, or another artist.

Legacy

Canaletto returned home to Italy to declining popularity. Art critics abroad had not treated him kindly. Many suggested that his artistic powers had fallen off. They said his style had become more rigid and predictable. His London paintings, they maintained, reflected a tendency toward monochromy—the use of varying tones of a single color. This, in their opinion, produced an uncharacteristic grayness in his work. The light and color of his earlier Venetian paintings was missing from his London works. Finely detailed, small figures that had once enlivened his views and landscapes had turned into hardly more than brushed-on blobs of afterthought. Such were some of the things that troubled Canaletto's London critics. Yet not every knowledgeable voice lamented his failings.

Eighteenth-century art historian Luigi Lanzi astutely observed that in Canaletto's paintings "the average spectator sees nature, while the connoisseur sees art. This he possessed in eminent measure."[1] Modern art scholar Alberto Cottino sees the absence of light and color in Canaletto's London works as nothing more than the differences in the environments of sunny Venice and not-so-sunny London. These variances are what Canaletto "strives to translate into his canvases. It is clearly not a matter . . . of a decline in his painterly abilities, as has been suggested more than once."[2] Further, the falling off of Canaletto's popularity can be attributed to other factors.

When Canaletto returned from England around 1756, the Seven Years' War was just beginning. The war arose over Austria's attempt to win back Silesia, which it had lost to Prussia in the War of the Austrian Succession. It involved most of the major powers of Europe and made traveling on the

Rome: The Arch of Constantine, 1742. Emperor Constantine I (c.280–337) built this arch in the fourth century to commemorate his victory over Maxentius. Canaletto chose the arch as the subject of one of five paintings of Roman subjects for Joseph Smith. Although the picture is viewed from the south side of the arch, the friezes (sculptured bands) and inscriptions actually appear on the north side of the arch.

continent both difficult and dangerous. Once again, a war had cut off the flow of visitors to Venice, and again Canaletto found clients for his works in short supply. Some scholars think that the shortage of tourists with money to spend on paintings made him turn from realistic *vedute* to imaginary *vedute ideate*—or *capricci*.

Canaletto had been producing *capricci* since his earliest years as a painter. Some of his favorite *capricci* featured Roman monuments. They originated during his brief stay in Rome from 1719 to 1720, and he referred to them often over the course of his career. He particularly favored the types of *capricci* that were based on real elements drawn from life. Canaletto took a piece here and a piece there and put them together. Like pieces in a completed puzzle, a picture of familiar elements emerged in a new and imagined setting. These he repeated many times in varying situations.

Representative *capricci* from Canaletto's last years in Venice include *Capriccio with Classical Ruins and Renaissance Buildings* and numerous variations on *Capriccio with Classical Motifs.* The painting *Classical Ruins* combined Roman architecture with Gothic and Renaissance structures. In *Classical Motifs,* the artist likely called on sketches recorded during his stay in Rome. He clearly based an arch in the background on the Arch of Constantine, which is located near the Colosseum. With more than twenty versions, this painting is one of the most often repeated compositions in Canaletto's entire body of work.

Joseph Smith remained Canaletto's friend. He sent new work his way as often as he could, yet even Smith could no longer find an outlet for all of the artist's work as he had in times past. Canaletto often had to find his own clients. One way he did so was to resume working in the open air, where he could be seen and approached by potential patrons. For example, John Hinchcliffe, the future bishop of Peterborough, was visiting Venice in 1760 when he saw "a little man"[3] sketching the Campanile of San Marco. He interrupted the artist and was thrilled to learn that he was Canaletto. The two men struck up a friendship. Canaletto gave Hinchcliffe the sketch, and the Englishman bought the related painting. Moreover, Hinchcliffe's traveling companion, a man named John Crewe, bought a spectacular view of London from the then-struggling painter.

As an interesting sidenote, Canaletto twice portrayed "a little man" sketching in his paintings. These miniature self-portraits appear in the left foreground of both *Old Walton Bridge* and *Rome: The Arch of Constantine.* His modest portrayals of himself bear out George Vertue's earlier observation regarding Canaletto's "reservedness & shyness in being seen at work, at any time, or anywhere."[4] Other artists of Canaletto's standing have treated themselves to much grander self-portrayals.

One of Canaletto's last clients was a German merchant named Sigismund Streit. He had come to Venice as a young man in 1709. Streit prospered over the next four decades and retired in 1750. The wealthy merchant had never married and was without heirs. He decided to leave the art collection he had assembled in his later years to his former school in Germany, the Gray Monastery Grammar School. In so doing, he hoped that a museum bearing his name would be opened there. His collection contained several *vedute* by Canaletto, among them *Grand Canal: Looking South-East from the Campo Santa Sophia to the Rialto Bridge* and *Campo di Rialto.*

Campo di Rialto, c. 1756, a view of the bustling activity of Venice's central market, is one of several paintings commissioned by Sigismund Streit, a wealthy German merchant. On the left side of the painting, Canaletto shows the Ruga degli Orefici, a street lined with the city's gold shops. Black-clad bank officials of the "Banco Giro" can be seen at work under the arcades at the end of the square.

Two of the paintings commissioned by Streit were nighttime scenes. They depicted celebrations held outside the churches of San Pietro di Castello and Santa Maria on the eve of the feast of their patron saints. These paintings were stunningly different but apparently did not please Streit. Of one, he complained: "In the painting of the Vigilia di Santa Maria all is not expressed in entirely as lively a manner as might be hoped. . . . On the sea itself there is not sufficient intelligence given of what the artist has beheld."[5] The disappointed merchant commissioned no more paintings from the aging artist.

In 1763, at age sixty-six, Canaletto applied for membership in the Venetian Academy of Fine Arts. His application was rejected, but he applied again

Architectural "Capriccio" with a Colonnade, 1765. Canaletto applied for membership in the Academy of Fine Arts in Venice several times before he was finally accepted as a member in 1763. Though acclaimed for his skills as a view painter, he somewhat surprisingly offered this *capriccio,* a study in perspective, as a precondition of his membership. The Academy appointed him Professor of Architectural Perspective.

later in the year. This time he was accepted. It remains unclear why the Academy rejected an artist as famous and talented as Canaletto. It probably had more to do with the kind of art Canaletto practiced than with the artist himself. Despite the popularity of view painting, it did not share the prestige of figure and traditional landscape painting. Also that year, he was appointed prior (head) of the *Collegio dei Pittori* (College of the Artists). Canaletto had at last received official recognition of his artistic achievements.

As a new member of the Academy, Canaletto was required to submit a reception piece. In 1765, he subtly abandoned *vedute.* Instead, he offered *Architectural "Capriccio" with a Colonnade* as his required offering. This view poses a study in perspective. It opens on a garden and another building.

Skillfully arranged uprights and diagonals lend increased depth to the picture. A vanishing point set in the lower right-hand corner of the painting reminds the viewer of a stage setting.

Scala dei Giganti, another canvas completed at about the same time, is similar to the Academy picture. Rather than an imaginary setting, it shows a real staircase in the Doge's Palace. It is probably one of Canaletto's last works. Little is known of Canaletto in the years beyond 1765. He continued to produce sketches and drawings, but no record of any paintings completed in his last years exists.

Canaletto died of inflammation of the bladder in Venice on April 19, 1768, at the age of seventy. He was laid to rest in a communal tomb in the church of San Lio, where he had been baptized. A very private man, he never married or made a will. Although his work was widely acclaimed and sought after in life, he left behind only a modest estate. To his three sisters, he left his house in the Zattere district, some furniture and jewels of small value, a little cash, twenty-eight unsold paintings, and some mostly worn clothes.

The true measure of Canaletto's worth lies in the body of his life's work—nearly 500 paintings and innumerable drawings and etchings. While many questions about the man and his private life remain unanswered, his work speaks for itself.

Perhaps biographer Anton Zanetti best summed up Canaletto's work in 1770. In his paintings, Zanetti wrote, the connoisseur

> finds great art . . . in the choice of sites, the distribution of figures, the handling of light and shade; and in addition, a lucidity and [pleasantly stimulating] facility of colour and of brushwork, the effects of a calm mind and happy genius.[6]

Canaletto's work inspired a host of successors—Bernardo Bellotto, Michele Marieschi, and Francesco Guardi, to name a few. Art scholars now recognize him as one of the most distinguished artists of the eighteenth century. His art brought light and air to Venice and light from another sun to London. In some small measure, the world became a warmer, richer place because Canaletto lived to paint. And that's not a bad legacy.

Joseph Smith

History recalls Joseph Smith as one of the great art collectors of the eighteenth century. His first passion was for book collecting, but it was his private collection of Canaletto's works that ensured his mention in the annals of art history.

St. Mark's, modern-day Venice

Joseph Smith was an Englishman. He was born in 1676 or thereabouts. Beyond his attendance at Westminster School, details of his early life have gone unrecorded. Around the start of the eighteenth century, he settled in Venice. He apparently earned his living as a banker, but he was also known as a good businessman. In about 1710, he married celebrated opera star Katherine Tofts. She was thought to be very rich and also subject to fits of madness that required her to be kept under restraint until her death in 1755.

Smith probably made his first contact with Canaletto in 1728. He commissioned a set of six views in or near the Piazza San Marco. A series of fourteen views on the Grand Canal followed in about 1729. These works established a relationship between artist and art collector/agent that was to last a lifetime. Today, they provide representative examples of Canaletto's early works.

In 1740, when demand for Canaletto's work declined, the ever-loyal Smith commissioned a series of Rome to help fill the void. Smith was appointed British consul in Venice in 1744. Two years later, when Canaletto left for England, Smith used his influence to help the artist find clients in London. Smith married again in 1758 but seems to have fallen on hard times shortly afterward. In 1762, he sold his collection of

St. Mark's (San Marco), modern-day Venice

Canaletto's work—over 50 paintings and almost 150 drawings—to King George III of England.

Joseph Smith died in 1770, when he was more than ninety years old. He was buried in the Protestant cemetery at San Nicolò al Lido. His patronage of Canaletto helped bring fame to Venice and beauty to the world.

1. *Grand Canal: Looking East, from the Campo San Vio*

2. *Piazza San Marco: Looking East*

3. *Grand Canal: From the Palozzo Balbi Toward the Rialto Bridge*

4. *Rio dei Mendicanti*

CHAPTER NOTES

Chapter 1. First Steps

1. J. G. Links, *Canaletto* (New York: Phaidon Press, 1994), p. 20.

2. Ibid., p. 26.

3. Terisio Pignatti, *Canaletto*, translated by Murtha Baca (Woodbury, New York: Barron's, 1979), p. 15.

Chapter 2. The Early Phase

1. J. G. Links, *Canaletto* (New York: Phaidon Press, 1994), p. 16.

2. Filippo Pedrocco, *Canaletto and the Venetian Vedutisti* (New York: Riverside, 1995), p. 26.

3. Ibid., p. 27.

4. Alberto Cottino, *Canaletto*, translated by Jeffrey Jennings (Milan, Italy: Electa, 1996), p. 7.

5. Ibid.

Chapter 3. Good Times and Bad

1. Terisio Pignatti, *Canaletto*, translated by Murtha Baca (Woodbury, New York: Barron's, 1979), p. 17.

2. Ibid.

3. Ibid.

4. J. G. Links, *Canaletto: Every Painting* (New York: Rizzoli, 1981), p. 6.

5. J. G. Links, author of introduction and descriptive texts, *Views of Venice by Canaletto engraved by Antonio Visentini* (Mineola, New York: Dover Publications, 1971), p. 3.

6. Pignatti, p. 18.

Chapter 4. The Artist Abroad

1. J. G. Links, *Canaletto* (New York: Phaidon Press, 1994), p. 165.

2. Ibid.

3. Adrian Eeles, *Canaletto* (London: Hamlyn Publishing Group, 1970), p. 11.

4. Links, p. 168.

Chapter 5. Legacy

1. Alberto Cottino, *Canaletto*, translated by Jeffrey Jennings (Milan, Italy: Electa, 1996), p. 13.

2. Ibid., p. 12.

3. Christopher Baker, *Canaletto* (New York: Phaidon Press, 2001), p. 23.

4. J. G. Links, *Canaletto* (New York: Phaidon Press, 1994), p. 168.

5. Dorothea Terpitz, Canaletto (Cologne, Germany: Könemann, 1998), p. 98.

6. Baker, p. 24.

1697 Giovanni Antonio Canal ("Canaletto") is born to Bernardo Canal and Artemisia Barbieri in Venice on October 28; baptized in the church of San Lio

1716 Begins training as a scene painter under his father

1719 Moves to Rome with his father to design and paint operatic stage settings

1720 Returns to Venice to paint *vedute;* becomes a member of the Venetian painters' guild

1722 Signs first contract with Owen McSwiney; uses the nickname "Canaletto" for the first time

1725 Stefano Conti commissions four paintings

1730 Joseph Smith, Canaletto's agent and client, commissions two of his paintings; McSwiney complains that Canaletto is late with his work and keeps raising his fees

1735 Giambattista Pasquali publishes engravings by Antonio Visentini of Canaletto paintings

1740 Searches for new subjects along the Brenta Valley with Bernardo Bellotto; Michele Marieschi publishes twenty-one Canaletto engravings

1742 Signs and dates five large *vedute* of Rome

1744 Bernardo Canal dies; Joseph Smith appointed British consul in Venice

1746 Arrives in London

1747 Paints important canvases for the Duke of Richmond; Sir Hugh Smithson (later Duke of Northumberland) commissions painting of Windsor Castle

1748 Begins painting views of Warwick Castle

1749 In sketches and *vedute,* documents repair work on Westminster Bridge

1750 Returns briefly to Venice; buys a house in Zattere district

1751 Returns to England

1754 Paints and inscribes paintings for Thomas Hollis in London

1755 Signs and dates *vedute* of the Old Walton Bridge; returns to Venice permanently

1762 Joseph Smith sells most of his Canaletto collection to King George III of England

1763 Elected prior of the Venetian Academy of Fine Arts

1765 Delivers reception piece to the Academy

1766 Inscribes his last dated work, a drawing of the interior of San Marco

1768 Dies in Venice on April 19; buried in the church of San Lio, where he was baptized

1770 Joseph Smith dies

1653 Oliver Cromwell becomes Lord Protector of England.

1660 Louis XIV of France marries Maria Theresa, daughter of Spanish monarch.

1669 Venetians lose Crete, their last territorial possession, to the Turks.

1679 Alessandro Scarlatti's first opera, *Gli Equivoci nell' amore,* is performed in Rome.

1687 Isaac Newton defines law of gravitation.

1693 William and Mary College founded in Virginia.

1697 Last remains of Maya civilization destroyed by Spaniards in Yucatán.

1707 England and Scotland form union under the name of Great Britain.

1714 D. G. Fahrenheit constructs mercury thermometer with numerical scale.

1721 Peter I proclaimed Emperor of All the Russias.

1732 Benjamin Franklin issues *Poor Richard's Almanack.*

1740 War of Austrian Succession breaks out.

1756 Seven Years' War begins.

1763 First permanent settlement at St. Louis (Missouri) established.

1775 American Revolution begins and lasts until 1783.

1782 James Watt invents double-acting rotary steam engine.

1787 French Revolution begins; it ends in 1789.

1799 Rosetta Stone is found near Rosetta, Egypt, enabling the deciphering of Egyptian hieroglyphics.

1800 U.S. federal offices move from Philadelphia to Washington, D.C.

1804 Napoleon Bonaparte proclaims himself Emperor of France.

1811 Jane Austen writes Sense and Sensibility.

1818 Border between the United States and Canada is set at the forty-ninth parallel.

1820 Missouri Compromise—Maine joins the Union as a free state; Missouri follows in 1821 as a slave state.

GLOSSARY

camera obscura (KAM-er-uh ob-SKYUR-uh)—Latin for "dark chamber"; a
darkened enclosure with an aperture, usually provided with a lens,
through which light from external objects enters to form an image of the
objects on the opposite surface.

capriccio (kah-PREE-chee-oh)—Italian for "caprice"; another name for
veduta ideata. Plural is *capricci* (kah-PREE-chee).

chiaroscuro (kee-ahr-uh-SKYUR-oh)—pictorial rendering in light and shade
without regard to color.

veduta (vee-DOO-tah)—Italian for "view"; a detailed, factually accurate
landscape, usually a cityscape showing buildings of interest. Plural is
vedute (vee-DOO-tay).

veduta ideata (vee-DOO-tah eye-dee-AH-tah)—Italian for "ideal view"; an
imaginary but realistic-looking view.

vedutista (vee-doo-TEES-tah)—Italian for a painter of *vedute*. Plural is
vedutisti (vee-doo-TEES-tee).

FURTHER READING

For Young Adults
While no other books have been written about Canaletto for this age group,
readers might enjoy these artist biographies from Mitchell Lane and other
publishers:

Ford, Carin T. *Andy Warhol: The Life of an Artist.* Berkeley Heights, New
 Jersey: Enslow Publishers, 2002.
Guzmán, Lila, and Rick Guzmán. *Diego Rivera: Artist of Mexico.* Berkeley
 Heights, New Jersey: Enslow Publishers, 2006.
Streissguth, Tom. *Mary Cassatt: Portrait of an American Impressionist.*
 Minneapolis: Carolrhoda Books, 1999.
Tracy, Kathleen. *Paul Cézanne.* Hockessin, Delaware: Mitchell Lane
 Publishers, 2008.
Whiting, Jim. *Claude Monet.* Hockessin, Delaware: Mitchell Lane Publishers,
 2008.
Whiting, Jim. *Vincent van Gogh.* Hockessin, Delaware: Mitchell Lane
 Publishers, 2008.

Works Consulted

Ainsworth, Claire. "Canaletto's Accuracy May Help Save Venice from a Watery Fate," *New Scientist Space,* October 18, 2001, http://space.newscientist.com/article.ns?id=dn1441&print=true

Baker, Christopher. *Canaletto.* New York: Phaidon Press, 2001.

Chilvers, Ian, Harold Osborne, and Dennis Farr (editors). *The Oxford Dictionary of Art.* New York: Oxford University Press, 1988.

Cottino, Alberto. *Canaletto.* Translated by Jeffrey Jennings. Milan, Italy: Electa, 1996.

Eeles, Adrian. *Canaletto.* London: Hamlyn Publishing Group, 1970.

Gayford, Martin. "How Canaletto Was Invented by an Englishman," *Telegraph,* May 11, 2005, http://www.telegraph.co.uk/arts/main.jhtml?xml=/arts/2005/11/05/bacanaletto05.xml

Links, J. G. *Canaletto.* New York: Phaidon Press, 1994.

———. *Canaletto: Every Painting.* New York: Rizzoli, 1981.

———, author of introduction and descriptive texts. *Views of Venice by Canaletto engraved by Antonio Visentini.* Mineola, New York: Dover Publications, 1971.

Martin, Gregory. *Canaletto: Paintings, Drawings and Etchings.* Boston: Newbury Books, 1970.

Pedrocco, Filippo. *Canaletto and the Venetian Vedutisti.* New York: Riverside, 1995.

Pignatti, Terisio. *Canaletto.* Translated by Murtha Baca. Woodbury, New York: Barron's, 1979.

Sewell, Brian. "A Tourist's Take on London," *Evening Standard,* January 29, 2007, http://www.thisislondon.co.uk/arts/artexhibition-20634150-details/Canaletto+In+England%3A+A+Venetian+Artist+Abroad+1746-1755/artexhibitionReview.do?reviewId=23383421

Terpitz, Dorothea. *Canaletto.* Cologne, Germany: Könemann, 1998.

On the Internet

Art Knowledge News: "Canaletto in England: A Venetian Artist Abroad, 1746–1755," http://www.artknowledgenews.com/Giovanni_Antonio_Canal-Canaletto.html

ArtsNet Minnesota: Environment, "Giovanni Canal (Canaletto)" http://www.artsconnected.org/artsnetmn/environ/canal3.html

Inside Scoop Kids: Canaletto. http://www.nga.gov/kids/scoop-canaletto06.pdf

Olga's Gallery: "Giovanni Antonio Canale, called Canaletto" http://www.abcgallery.com/C/canaletto/canaletto.html